BREA… G

BLANK

BY
DWAYNE
LAWSON-BROWN
AND REBECCA
BISHOPHALL

Peace Joshua Devine!
A pleasure to meet you
and hear your work.
The word is working with/
through you.
Dwayne B!

Book design by Shannon Pallatta

Early Response to *Breaking the Blank*

"Day Eight's *Breaking the Blank* delivers an engaging and fully relatable collection of poems by Rebecca Bishophall and Dwayne Lawson-Brown that carry us from childhood memories, first loves, and parenthood to the heartbreak of ultimate loss. The poets' relationship and culture-based poems reveal intimate life struggles while portraying resilient, real, and raw realities faced by many in today's society. Several of the beautifully crafted form poems brought me back for second readings as I recalled my own not dissimilar life journey. *Breaking the Blank* is a contemporary treasure for poetry readers and writers alike."

—Sistah Joy, Poet Laureate of Prince George's County, Maryland, USA

"This book feels like a rhythmic conversation that ricochets between old friends. As the poets share stories of parenting, single life, love, and the struggles of living from paycheck to paycheck, their poems sing and dance on the page. We share moments from the tenderness of waking up to laughter, the grittiness of being covered in vomit, and the ways we question our skills as parents ("how am I supposed to do it all/And not be delinquent as a dad?" Dwayne Lawson-Brown). The poets ask little of the reader but to listen and maybe sing, and perhaps dance, along."

—Susan Scheid, author of *After Enchantment*

"The poems contained within Rebecca Bishophall and Dwayne Lawson-Brown's *Breaking the Blank* are crisp, riveting, and often tender meditations on love, parenting, and—to paraphrase the title of a National Public Radio program—This African American Life. (For starters.) Sonnets, free verse and haiku consistently honor saxophonist Lester Young's credo: "You Got To Be Original, Man." They swing, and lament and celebrate. They are never mawkish or clichéd. (Somewhere Lester Young is smiling.) These poems are songs for the eyes, ears and heart. You'll replay them again and again and again."

—Reuben Jackson, author of *fingering the keys* and *Scattered Clouds: New & Selected Poems*

"Creating poetry is normally a solitary practice, so *Breaking the Blank,* a collaboration between Dwayne Lawson-Brown and Rebecca Bishophall, comes as a revelation. The collection pairs poems in conversation by each poet on facing pages, creating a dialogue on themes such as parenthood, money, poetry itself. "Write/To remember what it was like," Lawson-Brown says, and Bishophall responds, "The more pages the better;/read until I'm spent." These eloquent and necessary voices speak to each other and to us and we are compelled to listen."

—Gregory Luce, author of *Riffs & Improvisations,* and four other collections

"When the heart and the mind move together, words light up the sky. When we double that, with two poets, an Aurora empowers us, changing everything we knew before. This is a book to pick up, to read two good poems every day."

—Grace Cavalieri, Maryland Poet Laureate

"For. Real. That's what Breaking the Blank is. It is For. Real. These poems pulse with life, love, and all that is real. Dwayne Lawson-Brown and Rebecca Bishophall offer us a book stuffed with beauty. We get "Popeyes on MLK" and group chats. We learn why "her breath matters." We fall into the "mad rhythms" of "Double Dutch" and the heart fire of "Crush #1,062." We even learn how to "Love in the In-Between" and about the vomit that naturally comes with parenting. There are plenty of poems out there about far away worlds. But these poems are now, breathing, and real."

—Joseph Ross, Author of *Raising King and Ache*

Our Occupation

Is Existence

Is Parenting

Is Paying Bills and Taking Names

Is Feeling the Sun on Our Faces

Is Making It

Table of Contents

Breaking The Blank

Breaking The Mold

Parenting

Parenting
is being covered
in someone else's vomit,
but as long as they
stay asleep,
you won't move.

Cash And Respect

Popeyes on MLK sits; a crow's nest
Cawing echoes from my mom's checkered past
She held me close to her overgrown chest

Working register to make our meals last
I would cry at the sight of grease-filled pans
The skin sizzles, popped during standard tasks

The scars, polka-dotting her chestnut hands
From her, I learned work is an exercise
That we all must complete within this land

Set work ethic to ensure she'd provide
With thighs, fries, and biscuits baked; she made checks
For late evening toils meet daybreak's rise

To this day, on that Popeyes I reflect
How my mother made cash out of respect.

First Girl

A first girl
had a girl first —
loves books
and words.

She grew.

Learns and loves,
fears and falls…
In spite of,
she thrives.

In A Grand Way

She wakes up to laughter
Her little boy's little boy trying to play with daddy's hair
With that toddler's every chuckle
She feels the joy of being a successful mom
Forgets the sun setting on tarnished relationships
And basks in the sunrise of her little boy growing up

She wakes up to tears
Her little boy's little boy is potty training
Bathroom covered in streams of yellow
Even in the cleanup she smiles
Because when you cherish the things you take for granted
Dirty diapers become Picassos
The type of thing you can appreciate with your eyes closed

She wakes up to silence
Her little boy's little boy is sleeping
Her little boy is a grown man now
Her job as mother has been promoted in a grand way
Now she can finally go back to sleep
Without being bothered.

Our Love-ly Day

Love is "what's for breakfast?"
Breakfast cooked in the sunshine
Sunshine streams onto the sofa
Sofa becomes the place where we chat
Chat about jokes and games and music
Music quickly turns into a dance party
Party back to the kitchen in time for lunch
Lunch Munch Crunch
Crunch the numbers...time for a trip
Trip down the block for a treat
Treat ourselves to Slurpees
Slurpees that melt and become sticky
Sticky fingerprints all over the table
Table the next activity until we clean up
Up to you what movie we watch
Watch how you balance your plate!
Plate in the sink...time for a shower
Shower with kisses and tuck in tightly
Tightly I hold to these days and your love.

Twist For A Delinquent Dad

If I lie
And say I have a sitter
I do an injustice to my son
And am delinquent as a dad

If I book a sitter
And my sitter cancels on the day of
I still have to go to work
And am delinquent as a dad

If I don't book a sitter
And stay home with my son
I lose my job, can't afford food
And am delinquent as a dad

If I take my son to work
And he hobbles around on his crutches
I disobey the doctor's orders
And am delinquent as a dad

If I book a sitter
And I go to work as planned
I still miss out on time with my son
And am delinquent as a dad

If li... well... I....
And... you know, I don't know
I... but... how am I supposed to do it all
And not be delinquent as a dad?

Her Breath Matters

Rainbow-swirled spheres she
sculpts with breath made of giggles;
laughter floats on wind

She and I fight...still
hugs and kisses before sleep —
a must for good dreams

She still asks me to
lay with her; breath on my neck
helps me fall asleep

For The Growing Boy

When you were younger
You would sleep on my chest
I'd watch you rise and fall with each exhale
A reason for breathing

As you grew
You'd reached for my controller
Become player 2
Dream of making your own games
I pray we never outgrow our time

You grip the guitar neck
Like the world owes you your shot
It does
I will block anyone tending your goals

A father is proud of his son today
Everyday
E to A
Failure and success
You are my light
You are your own light

Keep shining.

Double Dutch

Just count her in
Up go her feet
Mad rhythm on the blacktop
Pride in her eyes
Ready to go again
Over the strings she flies
Perfect placement — she makes it look
Easy

Blank Space

Write — Right

Write
To remember what it was like

Write
Because every day is blank
No better ink than emotion

Write
On days when morning comes fast
And mourning comes easy

Write
For the wrongs
And our rights

Write
In beauty
And bitter lonesome ugly

Write
There will be a time
When the sand we are
Is all that is left

Seduction

Seduction…

Drag my finger down
their spine then
breathe them in.

The more pages the better;
read until I'm spent.

Tuesdays Are For Pretty

It's Tuesday and I'm answering the night's call
Slither from beneath blankets
Get gussied up
Put on my favorite dress
The yellow one that flows when I twirl
Hope that someone sees me and thinks
"Pretty"
With my ashy elbows and messy bun
My dirt-caked unwashed hands
A receipt for an afternoon of pulled weeds

It's Tuesday
And tonight is the perfect mix
Of lonesome and arousal
Find a place to share space
Before the cops shut it down
Or the price is too high for us to stay
Or the "right one" says the "wrong thing"
And we hear that familiar choppa song
Perfect weather to make a memory
With a stranger
And throw risk to the wind

It's Tuesday
Catch me twirling
Under bright lights
The prettiest boi in the streets.

Making Curfew

If I don't make it home in time
And get put out of the house
I will have nowhere to spend the night because I'm
out of money
And my phone has died.

I left Java Head early.
Something told me that 15 minutes can be a life saver.
I sped to get to the Metro station.
One: because it's freezing.
Two: because the train could betray me and come early.
Just in time,
I run up the escalator to grab a seat.
10:37.
Making good time.

I arrive at Metro Center.
"Please don't be 20 minutes till the next train.
Please don't be 20 minutes till the next train."
I sigh with relief as the monitor tells me 9.
I then take my seat on this train.
10:59.
Making decent time.

My journey is almost over and I'll be safe.
Worry-free until the next late night.
Then it hits me like an unexpected menstrual cramp.
Does the bus come at 11:43
or 11:34?

Suddenly my time has lessened to not good at all.
A glance at my watch lets me know I'm still safe.
11:26.
Sitting in the booth,
I begin to count the minutes.
The bus should be here at 11:41.
That will equal a 5-minute bus ride
and an 8-minute walk up the hill.
I'll be right where I want to be...on time.

11:38.
I'm getting my change out.
11:43.
I'm searching the horizon.
11:45.
I'm calling the house deciding to let someone know
I'll be late
when three rapid beeps fill me with dread.

My frostbitten fingertips can barely feel the power
button to try again.
Give me this one last call,
I silently plead.
I have just enough time to hear the beginning of the
answering service
over the rumble of the oncoming bus
and the night air being filled with my attempts at profanity.

Does the bus driver not understand
that since it is now 11:47
I am drastically behind schedule?
Is he going to find me somewhere to stay?

All I do is smile and drop in 35 cents.
Time is on my side.
It only takes 4 minutes to get to my stop.
But I've already come to the conclusion:

I gotta run.
There is no time to debate the issue.

I gotta run.
I put my purse in my bag,
make sure my keys and traitorous cell phone are
locked down.

I gotta run.
As soon as my foot hits the ground I'm OFF.
I don't care if people are going to have a story to tell
about how this crazy girl
high-tailed it off the bus
and ran like her life depended on it.

I gotta run.
This phrase has taken over the mantra of The Lord's Prayer
and The 23rd Psalm.

I gotta run.
This is what I say to myself as negative degree winds
snatch the breath from my lungs.

I gotta run.
There is no time to worry about boogeymen tonight.
They would have to catch me first.

I gotta run.
Unfortunately,
my bag and the fact that it's freezing outside prevent
me from sprinting all the way home.
I start to speed walk.
I glance at my watch.
11:53...
I gotta run.

With a last burst of speed,
I'm running,
past shadows I would have been scared of.
I'm running,
through wind that has caused snot to form in my nose.
I'm running,
on ankles that feel like Popsicle sticks.

I'm here.
I twist the screen door handle
only to realize it's locked.
No!
It's not locked!
I turned it the wrong way!

In the dim glow of the solitary street light,
I can't find the keyhole.
Desperation presses me to throw my face against
the door.
I'm in the house and the door is shut and locked
behind me.

11:58.
Everything is quiet,
except for the maddening cadence of my heart.

For Immortals That Live On Soundcloud

For Bryce

A simple "pardon me" would have been nice
As you bumped your way to heaven
Showing up at the gates
Before anyone saw your invitation

Never too soon or too late
Always on "God's time"

Sometimes God's time feels unfair
Like fate struck a clutch deal
Made off with the jewels and we left here
Wondering
"Why that bamma ain't text me back"
But his battery died
Permanent

Them defibrillator pads can't charge this
Charge it to the game
When your number's called, huh?
Gotta answer that call
Even when you dial it yourself

I always imagined it feeling like
Biting into a hard shell taco
But you got cavities...
Like that sharp prick
Close to a pinch on the inside

This shit hurts
So say excuse me at least!
Busting in line like we ain't get here first
All outta order… shoot…

What we 'sposed to do 'round here… live?

Wind Release/She's Grown So Thin

Can you feel the wind?
Light and buoyant.
Makes one feel like flying.
Try it.
The window's open.

She's grown so thin.
Her skin is stretched.
Her soul is showing.
You can see her heart beating.
Makes you wonder if she's eating.

She's grown so thin.
Is she sick?
Could be anorexic.
Waist getting small.
Barely nothing at all.

She's grown so thin.
Her mental state's not great.
Has she been feeling well?
She's always smiling.
How can you tell?

She's grown so thin.
She's been acting strange lately.
That much you know.
You decide to ask how she is.

Wait a second, where did she go?

A Mug's Dance

Coffee mugs
Sweating as they dance
To the cadence
Of excited conversation
The beads — banding at the base
Wedding the wood
A trace wetting to follow

The rings would work
Down to the edge of their table
Anticipating the next quip
Clopping as they are caught
Along the lip
Of syncopated speech
And lingering questions

The air won't be this crisp again
Until the sun demands distance
Mugs won't dance like this again
Until the fall.

His Inspiration

I

It's raining and cold
A basket of yarn stares at him
There's a poem here
He can feel it

A basket of yarn stares at him
It's much more demanding than thread
He can feel it
Gets the sudden urge to write

It's much more demanding than thread
A scarf begins to form
Gets the sudden urge to write
Picks up a pen

A scarf begins to form
Maybe 2
Picks up a pen
Fingers are flying

Maybe 2
It's raining and cold
Fingers are flying
There's a poem here

II

His tools lay before him
There's a poem here
Wants to catch it while he can
Gets the sudden urge to create

There's a poem here
A scarf begins to form
Gets the sudden urge to create
Threads under and across

A scarf begins to form
Maybe 2
Threads under and across
Now he needs to write

Maybe 2
Yarn turns into yarn
Now he needs to write
Fingers are flying

Yarn turns into yarn
His tools lay before him
Fingers are flying
Wants to catch it while he can

The Old Player's Lament

I want to play
But the game ain't what it used to be
Fingers just can't find the spots
To make a fine instrument sing

But the game ain't what it used to be
Maybe change is for the better
To make a fine instrument sing
A troubled song would be a weary blues

Maybe change is for the better
A dollar more — too rich for this blood
A troubled song would be a weary blues
Strummed by old bones on older roads

A dollar more — too rich for this blood
Saccharine sweet, molasses thick
Strummed by old bones on older roads
Paved with lust's toxic kiss

Saccharine sweet, molasses thick
And yes, I want to play
Paved with lust's toxic kiss
But fingers just can't find the spots.

Dream State

O to dream a normal dream
or simply lie awake —
where everything is as it seems
no further meaning to take;

No falling out of airplanes
or trapped inside an empty house;
no talking animals of any kind
leaping flames with no method to douse;

Just once to wake up surprised
by a completely empty slate;
no complicated images behind my eyes
teasing me about my fate;

For a normal dream, maybe counting sheep,
to quiet my imagination for a peaceful sleep.

Fill In My Blank

If lust was tangible
And you touched me
I would be on the verge of meltdown
And might surrender to thoughts unspoken

Crush: # 1,062

I think I kinda love you a little bit
When I see you my heart skips
And without us being intimate
You're mine
At least that's what I tell myself
When I read another line of your poetry
Pretending the girl that you're touching
Is me
And I'm laughing wittily
Instead you make me giggle nervously
How old am I, ten?
Even then I wasn't this transparent
Looking you over from head to toe
Wishing I'd done something more than cornrows
I hope you don't notice me subtly checking for funk
But it doesn't matter now
Because you just caught me checking out your junk
Obvious
I'm a head case
And I wish I could escape this place
The way my words escape me now
Your gaze unwavering
I want to make my intentions plain
But wouldn't you know it
Here comes the train
And we part

You with your gorgeous swagger
Me with my loudly thumping heart
In the beginning of this
I couldn't even speak to you
At least today was a start

Texting While Intoxicated

I haven't eaten all day
so this cider
has me slightly tipsy,
enough that I'm thinkin' 'bout it.

People will warn you about the drunk dial
but it's the drunk text
that will get you every time.
I go through a prolonged unlock/lock
routine with my phone.
It's been too long
and yet not long enough.
I still remember everything,
but have no recent memories.
Unlock.
Contacts.
Scroll.

I signal for another drink,
rum and coke this time —
the drink I order when I need clarity.
This will be the stupidest decision
I've ever made…
well, at least this month.
Cue up the type-delete routine.
Everything I want to say
has too much meaning for a text,
but I will be damned if I crack first
with the phone call.
Type it out, let it linger.

Signal for a third.
This time it's a shot.
You are the reason I don't drink tequila
and the reason I need it;
the reason I hate it
and why I will always remember the taste.
I miss you.
Send.

Of Smoke and Memory

Goldenrod streetlight
Humming over a black SUV
A road trip for the tethered
DC is in Brooklyn tonight
Soft thumb rushes
Over rugged flint
Sparked to pursed lips
This feels like home
Her hair and the smoke
Same color
Billowing like tunnel vents
On an empty side street
Can't believe it's not raining
In Gotham
The only wet I care for
Between her lips
A steam trap and
I'm lost in the clouds

A blown shotgun kiss
Leads to a blown shotgun love
A shotgun passenger
Leads to a shotgun wedding

This feels like home.

Three Little Words

"I missed you."
Your lashes touching,
lips move against my neck.
Not kissing,
just the slightest touch as you speak.
Your fingers
interlock with mine
and pull my hand
to your chest.
Skin warm to the touch.
Three pictures taken –
I still don't have enough words.
Fan on my back
gives me goosebumps,
but not the way your fingertips do.

If you don't breathe
and I don't breathe
I can imagine the world has stopped
and those three words will mean more than the three
other ones.

Honestly

I want to kiss you
urgently.
Wait, that was wrong.
I want to run my tongue
around your lips
and draw you to me with
unbridled passion.
But let's be real.
I can't do that.
Not because I have forgotten
how to kiss
or how to elicit passion.
I would hate to burn you,
to scorch you with the heat of
a thousand unfulfilled fantasies.
You on me, me on you.
Sometimes clothed,
sometimes as naked as the need on your face.
And let's be real.
I know you want me.
The thing you don't know is
I want you more.
Have wanted you since I first
saw you
and proceeded to undress you with my gaze.
I want to do nothing
but kiss you
24/7 —
until my lips are tingling like
they have fallen asleep,

only all of my senses are awake,
violently aware
of your hardness against my softness.
Your shoulders.
Your chest.
Your stomach.
I want to lay claim to all terrain
dark chocolate brown.
But let's be real.
No, let's be honest.
I could have you,
but I'm scared.
In fact as I write this piece
I'm nervous about you hearing it.
Nervous wondering whether
your breathing will grow short,
your hands will begin to clench,
and your mind will drift.
And let's be honest
(because you always are)
but unfortunately I'm not.
Because if I was honest
I wouldn't say I want to kiss you,
I would say I need to kiss you,
before I spontaneously burst from desire…
the desire that has been
rolling through me since I saw
your face.
I need you.
I want you.
Honestly.

Now kiss me.

Fresh Filet

If you got caught in my fishnets
And we turned the page in our tale
I don't know if you'd ever go home
And I'd have fresh filet on my tongue...

Don't ring my doorbell
I'm not strong enough to not let you in
With years of knocking and opportunities passed
If we bloom
This may be a blossom left unpruned
A timeline
A decade
A parenthood
A proposal en Flux
Don't knock on that door
Because what will we do
Other than fall
Like love is some cozy cove
And we aren't coven of pincushions
Bound for the prick

What is timing
In this catch and release romance
What if I want to hold your hand
And you don't want to let go

An Ideal or A Daydream

I.
You lease a house
With an option to own
On the coast
But far enough to not be
A hurricane risk

Your morning meditation
Seabreeze and sunshine
While the ocean meets your feet
White linen
Flowing like the few wispy clouds
Wandering what we call a sky

Your nights know
Perfect penmanship
Rum and want
The comfort of being free
There is a notepad
Singing your praises
There is a lover
That still tastes your breath
On their exhale.

II.

In a Southside townhouse
A ticket is purchased
To visit a lover
Who melts butter and barriers

A flight
To a coastal town where
The sun plays double-dutch with waves
An escape from home
To home
A familiar entanglement
A loosening of guards
A morning meditation
A moonlit stroll of rum and want.

Untitled 17

Somewhere in DC
there is a couch
in a basement
that still holds our butt-prints
as we sat shyly
under a fried chicken cloud.

I can feel you
watching me instead of "The Wire"
though I can't imagine
why.

The springs softly squeak
as you shift closer.

I turn only to meet your lips.

They taste like chicken.

Your hand lifts
then sets
lifts then sets
does this so often I take it
and place it on my waist.

You squeeze
and I playfully slap your
arm.

Back to Idris.

By the next commercial break
we are kissing
and your hand has shifted
to my thigh.

I have both of my hands
in your hair
and then run them over your shoulders.

Pause.

Before the screen goes black
with the upcoming ad
I've got my lips on your jaw
as you murmur something
unintelligible.

We kiss straight through
the end of the show
stopping only to change
rhythm.

It's time for me to go
and you drop me off with
the most chaste kiss of the
night.

My mother asks
why do I smell like Popeyes
when I was supposed to be
at the
movies

and
somewhere in DC
in a basement
a couch sighs in contentment.

Wake Up Apology

Wake up apology
Crawl from sleeping mouth
To beleaguered ears
What else can be offered to the wronged

If only we all could be as rested
On the morning after lashing
When best intention meets opposition
And solution — an olive branch burned

Apology
Do you come with company
Change
Or are you Easter chocolate-bunny hollow
A sickening sweet
Bound to hurt the whole

How do I hold you
Apology
With arms weak
Carrying the weight of misunderstanding
Bloodshot eyes strain to see the point in
"I'm sorry"
After a night of chasing thoughts
While you sleep on it

Be an answer
Be reason
Be more than
"My Bad" over mint and earl gray

Be strong
Double-shot espresso

A truth in the morning.

Pieced Back Together

Breaking
I was cracking
Split down the middle
My love told me
He didn't want to say "I love you"
Anymore
And would appreciate it
If I didn't say it either
My heart was
Breaking my heart

Cracking
I was split
Breaking in half
The next one didn't say it
Told me he had never said it
Was it even possible to feel it
I searched for ways he meant it
While telling him so in my mind
My drug wasn't
All he was cracked up to be

Split
I was breaking
Cracked irreparably
First I said it (he didn't)
Then he said it (I was indifferent)
Love was an earthquake and
Our faults
Caused more faults

Third split
Split my faith that love could be simple

You wonder why it's your responsibility
To arrange the pieces
That have been broken over and over
Jagged edges cut your fingers
And the sight of the blood frustrates you
Shards disguised as sharp words
I hate the pain they inflict
Don't want it to split us
I'm trying not to crack
Help me not to break again

Love In The In-Between

My partner wants to steal my dresses
Wear them around hips I long to hold close
She questions
What this makes her;
Why eyes linger on my legs
In stockings that accentuate what people use to define me
She loves the woman I hide inside
The way I love her;
Deep with want

Questions what this makes her
A kisser of queer body
Stroker of "them" in "him" trappings
Or simply a lover
In all the in-between

My partner sits in my closet
Rank with the stench of longing
And I
A pound of flesh worth the work.

Breaking The Cycle

Diasporic Hair

I have ugly hair
That breaks the unbreakable
Un-braid-able
A maze of a mess
Fingers pull hard to straighten the obstacle —
Coarse
Dark, brittle and dry
Unrefined
This hair is mine
I have real hair
Non-Synthetic — authentic — true
Slowly creeping from follicles like
Cotton pulled back by slave hands
Strands that mess with minds
Amaze
Shine in the dark
Absorbs grease with parts
Welcomes peppermint
Olive
Tea tree oils
Unrefined
This hair is mine
I have beautiful hair.

If I was alive in the 70s
And wore my hair like I did
I would have no reason to be embarrassed
And would shove a pick in my hair

Why Afros Are Cool

I walked in thinking
"I'm not a revolutionary,
and I have no aspirations to be one."
I hope there's no fist pumping,
or screaming of
REVOLUTION!
My newly afroed hair
scratches my ears and
I can't help but wonder how they put up with it.
The only reason I do this,
is to win prizes.
The scarf's lopsided bow
is in a state of defiance.
It will not be considered "borrowed
from a white girl
whose style is so different from mine,"
but only "borrowed from a friend."
The fro stands alone,
sadly.
I expected more competition.
Not a night of homogeny.
I look around
and see all types of faces.
All here
I worry
to shout

REVOLUTION!
I nervously tuck the strands of fro around my ears.
Poems about:
Women,
Men,
Identity,
Survival,
Hip hop,
Spirituality,
Jane.
Afterwards, chicken
and politickin'.
To my left,
an informal caucus on
how to do this better next time.
To my right,
the Latina Leaders of the Future
plotting their next big attack.
Suddenly I feel comfortable,
but comfortable in a way
that allows me to forget
I look crazy with this floppy mess of hair
on my head.
Couldn't even call it a real fro.
And in the
REVOLUTION!
you gotta keep it real.
Impromptu games of fooz ball.
At each score I pump my fist in the air.
My partner,
whom I've never met before,
gives me a high five.
And the

REVOLUTION!
all makes sense.
All they wanted us to do was understand the differences.
Something has been accomplished here tonight,
and it isn't the taming of the fro.
It's the combined effort to do a thing worthwhile.

Sun and Shade

The day is sunny
And DC is still taxed
While the Mayor parades
Pageantry and circumstances dire
In the district
People
Somewhere between
Ugly riches and polished poverty
Celebrate the freedom
To gather on stolen land
And DC is still taxed
Territory — citizens without a voice
Represented by shadows
A shaded city
Deserving of so much more.

Sunlight breaks through
Cherry blossom trees
Peak bloom
The same length
As patience with the system
And DC is still taxed
And her people still tasked
Assigning responsibility to those
In charge of making changes
A shaded city
Trying to step into the light.

Playground Pause

Cops
near
playground
turn laughs to
silence. Adults still
until the lights turn the corner.

Pain Per Due

You'll walk into a faux French bistro on the waterfront
The type of establishment shoehorned in to cater to travelers
Looking for cultured meals in cookie-cutter pre-planned
urban redeveloped safety
This is not your usual flavor
But today is for budding
And you have good taste

You are a native here
Ran these roads during gym class drills
Carried large bushels of crabs
For steam and smoke sessions at Aunt Mae's
Ducked niggas looking to snatch your shoes
And hid behind trees in what used to be the park.

It's now a CVS
Convenient. Valuable. Serviceable.

You walk in
One of 3 brown faces
The only one not in formal wear
Zebra-print shoes
Bangles and green tipped locs
Adorn your small but growing frame
The staff
Off-guard when you order the "Pain Perdu"
With perfect diction
There is no tree to hide behind now

Embarrassment and prejudice

Go down easy
With blueberry compote
The French toast
Sweet as erasure
The tab
Covered in the price of my past.

Obligatory Black Poem

Without fail
The Uber driver asks
"Where are you from?"
DC
Southeast
Family from VA
They want to know origins
A road map to bloodline

I'm Black
Black like claiming every culture because so few claim me
Black like not knowing the answer but you got a hunch
Like "ji like" knowing
Jive Turkey
A country blues duty whine Black
Patois back-alley hooch Black
Like "my sorrows don't know how low I been"
That chariot better be swangin'
Better be sweet
Like that blackest berry
And just as obsolete

Black

Unlike snow
More like pavement
Forward motion
Black like cool
Cold
Black ice

'Cause slick be a second language
And twice as rich as fossil fuel
Black

You know
Like truth
Little white lies
Let White men run in
Big white buildings
Let White men run big white buildings
Let White women defy law and find martyrdom
I'm Black as honesty
Like "nah moe"
Harsh but real Black
Like mom nicknaming you stinky cause you stink
Like "let me know you're home safe for real"
Like forgetting
The absence of memory
Black hole space and time
Black holds space and time
Like the beginning of
Black
Like time
Black
A starting point
A finale
Black

Like "I dont know what fucking country
Damn"
Black as being from America
But never feeling safe enough to claim it

Knowing sometimes it ain't some shit to claim
Voted for change
Voted for the same
Black
Like the only black I see in school is the board
And that was replaced with something white
Black as my son
Accent on white linen of catholic school classroom
Black box checked in digital headcount
Like surviving
And succeeding
And playing their game while making his own

Black
Like Kristen in Connectivity
And Monique in Youth Services
Anita spittin' them poems
And Kamala in Eisenhower Executive Office
And Wesley Snipes in Blade
And Wesley Snipes in Tax Court
And Black as me
In this motherfuckin Uber
Because I still can't hail a taxi.

Just trying to make it home safe
And remember to let someone know.

Make It Make Sense

How did police decide on red and blue
Primary colors without the yellow
"Protect people" — I believed to be true

When I was her age and still felt mellow
About the people with guns on their hips
From serious stares to waving hello

Many hashtags have made me come to grips
With the fact some don't care about my life
Behind me in traffic and my heart skips

Yet I do not want her to know that strife
So some of these thoughts with her I won't share
As long as possible, have a child's life

I still am torn — do they or don't they care
Realizing soon, she will become aware

The Good Side

And the shots rang out
While I host an open mic
And the audience won't know the terror on this side
Can't relate to this Black
This fall in the winter
With sirens
Flashing like life and gunpowder

They say I'm on the good side of the south side
Of this Black
And the shots rang out

Tonight
I sleep under blue and red lights
Double-dutching between warped blinds
The sounds of us
Reliving terrors
Releasing the world and finding an after
My ears don't know silence
I mourn for those hit
And prepare to spit
And none of them will know

They don't know this Black
On the good side.

On Scoring The Big Win

What does it look like
To win in a city with
Rules that change like times?

We Scribble Our Time
On Any Scraps We Can Claim,
Proof That We Were Here.

Our Stories Live On
In The Pages Of Books, Our
History made flesh.

From the blood of my
Lineage to the flavor
On My Tongue – well red

Just because eyes can't
See the lie, it doesn't mean
Hearts Can't Feel The Truth

Take a deep breath. Hold
It. Feel The Strain. Now breathe. Life
Is Within The Return

Undeniable
Loyalty, Framed With A Smile
That Dribbles With Love.

Soft As Baby Yawns
The Beauty Of New Life Sits

Unmatched, Unaltered.

In A Capitol
City, We Slap Sticks against
Ice and Score Big Wins

We Roll Forward, Led
Along Our Path; Spinning Spokes
To Reach This Life's Goal

Crafted with love and
Warmth; like a hug you can wear;
Flavor of Family

We Claim Love Like A
Neighborhood. Stitch Together
Our Hearts And Come Close

More Than Holding Hands,
Sharing Space and Time, Love Is
Owning All Your Faults

Knowing Your Strengths and
Being Held Accountable
For Your Shortcomings

Many Faces, One
Room. Many Lifestyles, One Goal
Unified For Youth

To Know The Fear And
Still Speak Up – That Is Courage.
In Spite Of Judgment.

Every Word Spoken,
Bold As Truth – Heartfelt And Clear
"From The Mouth Of Babes..."

A generation
Of youth kicking the odds in
The face. That's Winning!

Breaking The Rules

BC

It costs me 10 dollars a month
to remain childless,
but recently,
I've been wanting to waive that fee;
even though
10 dollars is such a small
price to pay for sanity.

I become baby crazy
when I forget to take my meds —
BC without the BC
and what I sleep on becomes
more than a bed,
it becomes a vessel for wishes unspoken,
because when he gazes into my eyes,
I want him to just be able to tell.

The air is filled
with my hormones
and I've taken to wearing pheromones
so when he smells me
he wants to jump my bones
but won't know why.

This is not a trap.
It's just that lately
I'm feeling a little past my prime.
In earlier times,
a woman my age
would have had at least four kids

already,
aged two through nine.
I feel behind
and had taken to crying
in my room, door locked,
my mother thought I was dying.
Had to convince her I was fine.

Last week,
I was thrown out of CVS;
not because of a theft,
but because I had rubbed
baby lotion all over my arms
and was smelling myself.
Told the security guard I wanted
to smell fresh
and Zest
wasn't cutting it.
I went home and downed
an entire week's worth of
ortho-tri-cyclen
and it worked...
until I went to the park and saw little babies
tri-cyclin'
and slide climbin'.
I just wanted to take five of them
home with me
but that would be a felony.
Need to get back on the BC
before I'm in the penitentiary
serving twenty to life.

I used to think I had to be someone's wife
before I became a mother.
I don't feel that way anymore.
All I want to get is that teething ring.
Funny how such a small thing
can bring such happiness.
I'm anxious to be blessed
with one of my own;
until then I take another pill to the dome
and wait.

A Little Disarray

My hair
Ain't done
Nothing to nobody
So why do they want to do so much to it?
Cut it
Burn it
Bleach it as if the length
Texture
Color has anything to do with them
As if things can live without pigment
Repelling the sun
Demand I bind it in clips
Clip it with clippers
Snip it with scissors and leave it behind
Plucked like black cauliflower
Bunched along the floor
My texture is a maze
Inching it's way to the heavens
Hiding how heavy the crown is
How strong the shoulders are that bear this world
My texture is a maze
Meant to keep intrusion at a minimum
And heat at max
My texture is amazing
And no you may not touch it

If you think my hair's a mess, wait till you see my heart
And if my heart ain't too messed up, can you handle
 my thoughts?
'Cause everything up there's a little bit in disarray

And that pales in comparison to what I'm 'bout to say

Masculinity is so fragile
Because it begins with a mask
Meant to be broken
Even the latex ones
Ripped and torn through like condoms
Used to mask the sex
Used to hide the daddy's true identity
Broken because he probably put it on backward
Inside out
Face to face
Couldn't handle the pressure and
Torn
Like an ego
When not top priority in someone else's timeline
When not being checked for
When she don't let you check up on it
Check yourself man!
You don't own anyone
Everyone needs time and space
No person is a black hole

If you think my hair's a mess, wait till you see my heart
And if my heart ain't too messed up, can you handle
my thoughts?
'Cause everything up there's a little bit in disarray
And that pales in comparison to what I'm 'bout to say

Love is mid-afternoon naps
Love is fresh brick-oven baked pizza
In huge slices
It's cold beer and warm bodies

It's better than the circumstances
It's helping you get through them
Love isn't the diamond
It's the fixture holding the rock in place
My love is soooooo big
It created the universe
All this blackness was just sitting there
My heart was so full it just BANG
My love is creation
It's science
It's understanding
It's logical
Love isn't logical
Doesn't check the balances
Just writes the check
Would sign away the day if to buy another time
Love pays
My love is busy
And distant,
My love got bills to pay
A mouth to feed
My love has a wallet and bank account
Neither of which stretch
My love is a ball of yarn
Knotted
Twisted
Unraveling
Could be useful if someone with some knowhow had
  patience for the patchwork
My love
Knows fiber work is a dying art

If you think my hair's a mess, wait till you see my heart
And if my heart ain't too messed up, can you handle
my thoughts?
'Cause everything up there's a little bit in disarray
And that pales in comparison to what I'm 'bout to say.

The Twist: If I could have one wish
and nothing more
I would want the ability to deliver the hotness
and burn down all the open mics.

I Want To Be A Poet

I want to be a poet.
I want ink to flow in my veins
and words to flow off my tongue;
to command audiences with
my impressive vocabulary
and master the art of wordplay.
I want my favorite food
to be pen tops
and my favorite performer to
come out with a new fragrance:
Eau du Looseleaf.
I want to be a poet.
I want to need it,
to be restless without it,
to be searching for a pen
the way smokers look for cigarettes;
to be constantly finding rhythm
in everyday conversation
and be able to phrase it in a way
that's immortal.
I want to be a poet,
but let me be specific:
I want to be that poet.
I want to be the poet
who spits their first line,
half the audience already knows it

and starts snapping.
I want to be the poet
who has at least two pieces of
paraphernalia on sale,
at the same time,
and one that's out of stock.
I want to be the poet
who knows all the other poets
and their poet friends
and we've all written a piece together.
I want to be the poet
who engages men and women
and not just when I'm talking about
copulation.
And I would be a poet
who makes the newcomers realize
it's not about quantity but quality,
not mediocrity but mastery,
not ignorance but intelligence.
I want to be a poet —
and maybe if I say it enough times
I will be.

If I had unlimited quantities of money
And didn't have to pay any debts
I could stop dodging calls from bill collectors
And wouldn't feel so poor

Recession

I owe my mother 200 dollars
every two weeks for rent
and if I'm off by a cent
she finds
and fines me
a dime for every time
I give her a line
about needing this new tee.

And there ain't no way
I'm dealing with Sallie Mae.
You can tell that heifer
I ain't got it
and if she don't believe me
she can look in my wallet.

Matter of fact,
I'm ducking all phone calls
which shouldn't be too hard
'cause my phone's been turned off.
Cingular has considered me
too much of a liability
and given me a break.

Want to go to the movies and relax
but that ain't a piece of cake.

It costs nine if you want a seat
another six if you want a snack
and the last time I checked out nacho prices
I almost had a heart attack.

I'm trying to put away some money to save.
The effort feels like it's putting me in an early grave
because between hair appointments and my insurance
laundry and new clothes
I find myself borrowing money from
which one and who knows.
And it's getting pretty frustrating
always having to duck and dodge
plus it doesn't help when all I hear is
"don't you have a good government job?"

Does anyone know how I can become friends
with some high-rollin' ballers?
Oh, you got some people I need to meet?
Great,
until then let me hold five dollars.

What's the Matter

The issue is I'm broke
And broken
And stitching together a life with
Cardboard and wet yarn

And I'm busy
And bothered
While trying not to be a bother
In these bothersome times

See I'm tired
And tied
To a tireless age
I'm watching the world
And what I say
And say
The world watches my every move
The way I work
Make the streets a sweatshop
My hands — faculty and factory
My mouth — a machine
Syllabic syntax produced

Even in death my body works
Carrying the stigma of
Black
Queer
Parent
The motion of stillness
Busy body it is

With all this existing
It's amazing it can still find a moment for meals

And the buzz is deafening
The chatter of a world too hungry
To enjoy its feast
Clamoring for the next bite
As it chokes down another life

I refuse to be eaten today
Won't be swallowed or chewed
I remain whole
Mealy morsels to share if I choose
In this moment
I claim a stillness only mountains know
One in presence and motion
Foundation in rotation

Today I will not be moved.

Untitled 57

I haven't wanted to dance
Under strobe lights
Crushed between bodies
On a sticky floor
With a drink in hand
And bass beat in chest
In too-high heels
Frenetically
Energetically
Laughing too loudly
Sweating profusely
And not caring
In so long

But now I'm dreaming of it.

Rage and Release

Its 2021 and I'm fucking old
Like "gray in the beard and the locs
Annoyed that my phone wants to autocorrect my hair"
Old
At a hard-core show
Under red and purple lights
And the rage is real
The want to crash into someone and feel something
  other than
Wanderlust and envy

The guitarist growls
Like a pissy mattress
Begging for a flip
And it happens
Orange Hoodie starts thrashing
And we collide
All sweat and frustration
Callous and care
Hurt me
But know my mend

I've always wanted
To love like a rave
To fuck like a mosh pit
To feel and get felt
Reciprocity

In a pandemic
We hurt together

And tonight
We care to make sure
We each leave breathing.

Notified

WordPress notification: 8:43AM — John Arrington liked your post "New Posts — No April Fools"

Mornings sit on chest
Weighted blanket on a cotton-filled lonely
Friday
And twilight clips between the blinds

Email notification: 8:51AM — Hey Dwayne B! Something on your wishlist is now on sale in the Nintendo EShop!

And it is
As awaking can be
Rude and abrupt
Vibration and restless
Everyday
Still Life
Screening screens
In isolation

Text Notification: 9:20AM — Ignore

A stutter stop
Taciturn tantrum
From a pachyderm roommate

Call From Scam Likely: 10:34AM — Ignore

Wanting
Seems selfish

Outside
Seems selfish
Missing you
Seems...

Voicemail Notification: 10:35AM — 20 seconds of white noise

Selfish

And the day doesn't mind
A meandering mind
Wanderlust personified
Here does not feel like...

Facebook Message Notification 11:46AM — 3 unread

A derailed train
Is a thought deferred
A virtual memory
Wiped
A filthy clean
For the unrecalled

Zoom Meeting: 12:30PM — 1 of 3

A pachyderm returns
Makes seat of chest
A quilt of questions
And...

Text Message Notification: 1:37PM Lawson-Brown Men Group Chat — 1 of 6

I'm safe
Which is to say
Death has yet to know my address
The bullet was not mine
Today
And all cars stayed their course

Mourn the lost
Celebrate the life
Recognize the Causes

Pachyderm Roommate

Instagram Notification: 2:12PM 4 of 16 — Unread

I just want to…

Facebook Message Notification: 2:13PM 4 Unread

…Think…

Microsoft Teams Meeting Reminder: 2:15PM —
Meeting begins in…

without the pressure

Pinterest Notification: 2:16PM

of

Yahoo Email Notificati…
Gmail Notific…
Twitter Noti…

Buzzing

Instagram Live Notification: 5:30PM — Online Trivia Party

And I am buzzing
And streaming
Turned on and digitized
For consumption
Product
Posted
Unsold

Paypal Notification: 6:37PM — Payment sent to Smi...

When it dies
All is still
But the thoughts
Scampering the minds floor
Calls missed
City in peril
Son alone

And all is still

But the locs that won't fall
And the resilient ash
Hunkered between my thumb and pointer
Pen swaying — A meter bump on the green line
Signs of life
All still

In motion.

Adulting

Adulting is not for the weak
there is so much I need to do
everyday before I can sleep
overwhelmed constantly always;

Don't consider myself strong but
adulting is not for the weak
I have to keep moving forward
pushing pulling myself along;

Tried complaining to a friend
but they simply shrugged and then said
adulting is not for the weak
and left me alone with my thoughts;

It won't get any easier
there will be times I want to quit
those times I will whisper softly
adulting is not for the weak.

Untitled 46.202.2

I am not
Finished

I am not
A run on sentence

I am not
The answer

I am not
The problem

I am not
A failure

I
Have fallen behind

I
Am hurt and healing

I
Am trying

I
Am dizzy and worrying and fighting the mold
Working, creating, and taking control

I
Am shard and shape

The scattershot
Burst and shatter

I
Am still here.

Fail, Don't Quit

I am failing
but haven't quit
trying to make things fit
without bailing.

Nothing comes from wailing
move forward bit by bit
I am failing
but haven't quit.

My courage is ailing
confidence continuously taking a hit
glancing down into the pit
but my fingers are curled around the railing
I am failing
but haven't quit.

ABOUT DAY EIGHT

Day Eight's vision is to be part of the healing of the world through the arts, and our mission is to empower individuals and communities to participate in the arts through the production, publication, and promotion of creative projects.

Day Eight's programming includes an online magazine, poetry events, live arts programming, book publishing, arts journalism, and education programs for children and youth.

Example 2021 projects include:

The DC Arts Writing Fellowship was created to support early career arts writers. The project is conducted in partnership with local news outlets including Tagg Magazine and The DC Line. An annual conference brings together leaders in the field of arts journalism.

The DC Poet Project is a poetry reading series and open-to-all poetry competition that supports the professional practice of poetry. The 2020 instance of the DC Poet Project was produced through support from the Wells Fargo Community Foundation and the National Endowment for the Arts.

Day Eight's projects in local art history included an online archive dedicated to DC's first artist cooperative gallery, the Jefferson Place Gallery.

All of Day Eight's projects are made possible by the support of volunteers and individual donors, including the Board of Directors. To learn more about the organization please visit www.DayEight.org.

Day Eight